Level 2

The Nature Kid's Guide to

BEARS

RENATA MARIE

LP Media Inc. Publishing
Text copyright © 2023 by LP Media Inc.
All rights reserved.

For information address LP Media Inc. Publishing,
3178 253rd Ave. NW, Isanti, MN 55040
www.lpmedia.org

Publication Data

Bears
The Nature Kid's Guide to Bears — First edition.

Summary: "Learn all about Bears, the Nature Kid Way"
— Provided by publisher.

ISBN: 978-1-954288-63-8

[1. Bears – Non-Fiction] I. Title.

Title: The Nature Kid's Guide to Bears

CONTENTS

BEAR COUNTRY

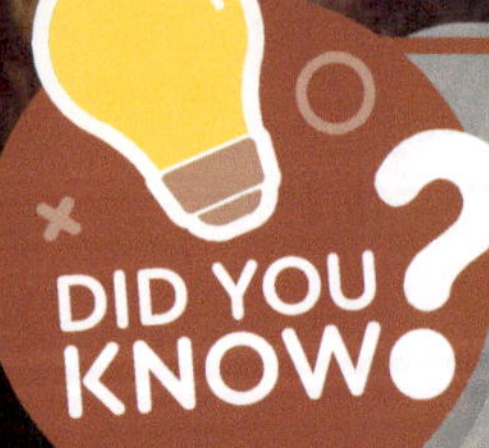

There are eight types of bears in the world. There are brown bears, black bears, polar bears, giant pandas, moon bears, sun bears, spectacled bears, and sloth bears.

Sharp teeth show. Long claws rip. A bear charges.

There are three types of bears in North America. Brown and black bears live in forests. They look for food under the trees. Polar bears live on the ice. They walk through snowstorms to find food. These are no teddy bears. They are big. They are hungry. And they are on the hunt.

Brown Bear

Black Bear

Polar Bear

Giant Panda

Moon Bear

Sun Bear

Spectacled Bear

Sloth Bear

BIG BEARS

BLACK BEAR
UP TO
600 POUNDS
(272 KG)

BROWN BEAR
OVER
1,000 POUNDS
(454 KG)

POLAR BEAR
UP TO
1,700 POUNDS
(771 KG)

A polar bear stands on his back legs.

Polar bears are the biggest bears in North America. Their big bodies help them stay warm.

Brown bears are a close second. Gaining fat helps them sleep through the winter.

Black bears are the smallest. Being small helps keep them safe. If they see danger, they can quickly climb a tree.

Female bears are usually smaller than males.

Polar bears can be over 11 feet (3.4 meters) tall when they stand on their back legs.

BUILT TO HUNT

A bear sniffs for food.

Bears are built to find prey. They are built to attack. Bears have sharp noses. They can smell animals that are far away. They have small, round ears. They have sharp hearing. They can see well.

Bears have powerful bodies. They have strong legs. Their paws are large. Their claws are strong. Their teeth are sharp. One swipe or bite and the prey is theirs.

BIG BELLIES

DID YOU KNOW?
Bears will go into towns when they cannot find food. They eat farm animals. They eat trash.

A nose sniffs. A belly rumbles. A bear is hungry.

Bears are omnivores. **They eat meat and plants.** Each type of bear eats what it can find.

Polar bears live where it is icy. They eat seals, birds, fish, eggs, seaweed, small animals, and berries. They even eat walruses, narwhals, belugas, and reindeer.

Brown and black bears live where there is more food. They eat berries, grasses, fruits, flowers, nuts, fish, bugs, and small animals.

They sometimes hunt larger animals. They hunt young elk, caribou, deer, and moose. They even eat dead animals.

ICE FISHING

A polar bear watches a hole in the ice. *Splash!* It's a seal!

Polar bears mainly eat seals. Seals breathe air. They swim up to holes in the ice. Bears sniff for the holes. They walk quietly to the edge of the ice. They stay as still as they can. And they wait.

When a seal pops up, the bear attacks! It reaches with its long neck. It sinks its teeth into the seal. And it uses its strong body to pull the seal onto the ice.

Polar bears have white fur. It helps them hide from seals on the ice.

SWIMMING
UPRIVER

A brown bear crashes through a river. He stomps and claws. He pins a fish.

Brown bears hunt in many ways. They stand in rivers. They catch fish as they jump out of the water.

Brown bears charge their food. **A strong hump on their backs helps them run fast.** They can run up to 35 miles (56 kilometers) per hour.

The hump also helps them dig. With their long claws, they move dirt. They pull up plants and bugs.

Adult brown bears rarely use their claws to climb. They are usually too big for the trees.

QUICK CLIMBERS

Curved claws dig into bark. A black bear cub races up a tree.

Like brown bears, black bears use their claws to find food. They rip open logs. They turn over rocks. But they also use their claws for something else.

Black bears can climb. They look for food in the high branches.

High in the trees, they are safe from **predators**. Mountain lions, wolves, bobcats, and coyotes hunt black bear cubs. They even have to watch out for other bears.

Black bears can climb 100 feet (30 m) in 30 seconds.

STRONG SWIMMERS

Polar bears can swim at
six miles (9.7 km) per hour.

Big paws splash through the water. A polar bear is swimming.

Bears swim to find food. They swim across rivers and lakes. Polar bears even swim across the sea.

Polar bears have big paws. Their front paws pull at the water. Their back paws help them turn. Their bodies are long. Their necks are long. They easily cut through the water.

Their fur keeps the freezing water out. Their fat keeps them warm. It also helps them float.

Polar bears can swim for days at a time. They rest on floating ice. They can even swim for 62 miles (100 km) at a time.

BEDTIME SNACKS

The leaves change to gold. The air grows cold. Winter is coming.

In the fall, bears eat a lot of food. Black bears can gain four pounds (1.8 kg) a day. Brown bears can gain six pounds (2.7 kg) of fat each day. Soon, they will go to sleep.

In winter, there is less food. Bears dig dens and they fall asleep.

Some bears can sleep for eight months. They usually do not eat. Their fat keeps them alive. They can lose one-third of their body weight.

Sometimes, bears can go all winter without pooping or peeing.

ICE WALKERS

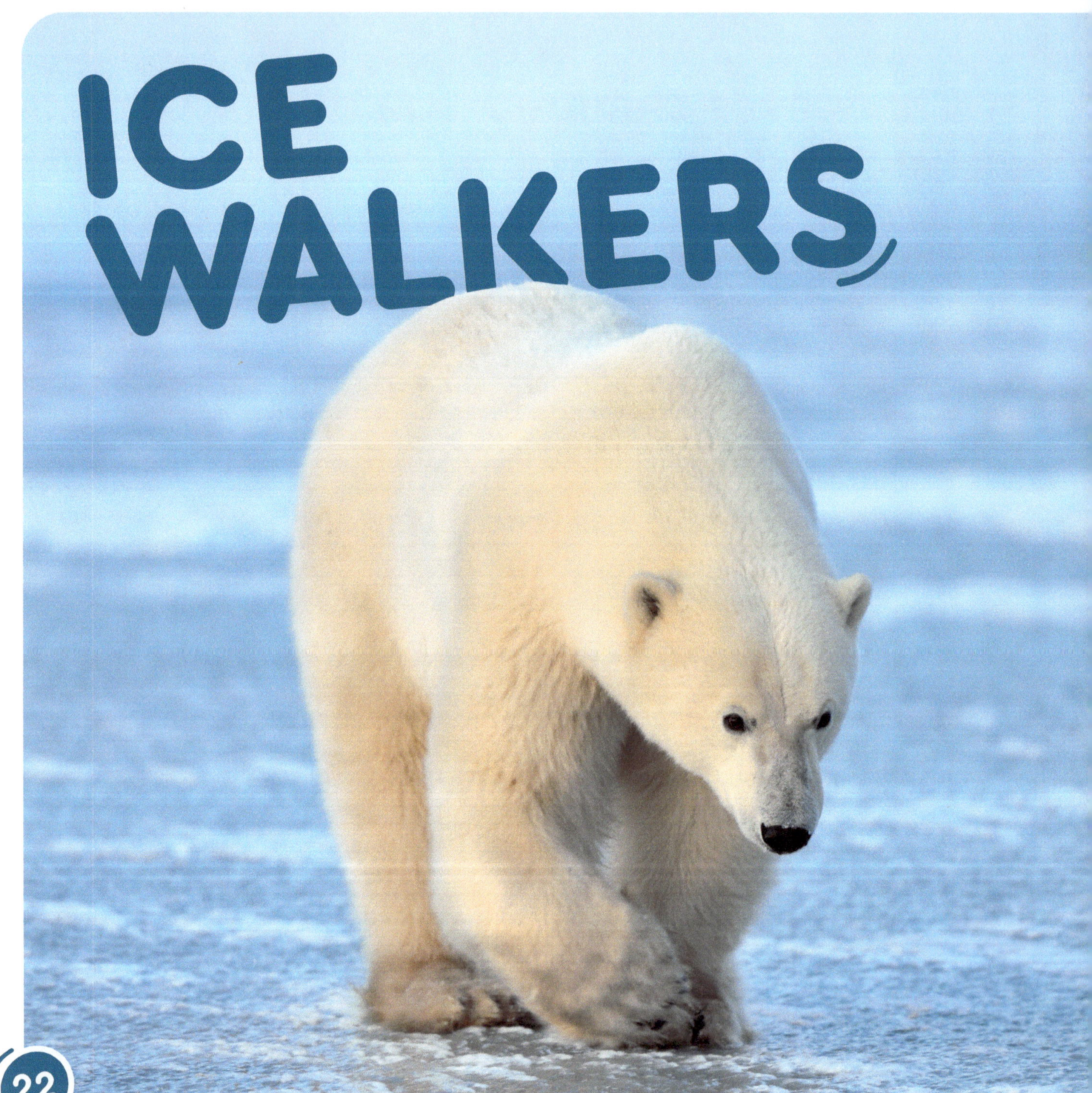

Ice forms. Snow flies. But a polar bear keeps walking.

Polar bears do not sleep through the winter. They must move to where the food is.

In the fall, the sea freezes. Polar bears live on the ice. They hunt for seals.

In the spring, the ice melts. The sea turns into open water. There is less ice to hunt seals on. Polar bears swim to the land to find food.

CUDDLY
CUBS

Little balls of fur sleep in a den. They are baby bears.

Baby bears are called cubs. Most mother bears have two to three cubs at a time. Cubs are born in the winter. They are born blind. They are almost hairless.

Mother bears clean their cubs. They feed them milk. Bear cubs hum while drinking. Their mother keeps them warm. Cubs are safe in their dens.

Mother bears eat their cubs' poop. It keeps their dens clean and keeps predators away.

26

Snow melts. Flowers grow.
A little nose sticks out of a den.

Cubs leave their dens in the spring. They roll and **wrestle**. They bite and play. They are learning to fight. They are growing stronger.

Cubs watch their mothers. They copy her. They try to hunt as she does. They learn how to find food.

For a few years, they will need their mothers to teach them and keep them safe. Even from other bears.

Black bear cubs grow fast. They can weigh 80 pounds (36 kg) by their first birthday!

STAND AND FIGHT

A bear stands on his back legs. He is ready for a fight.

Bears fight for food. Male bears fight for females. **When bears fight, they want to look big.** They fluff up their fur. They stand on their back legs.

The bears **growl**. They bite. They swipe their giant paws. They wrestle each other to the ground.

Whichever bear comes out on top wins.

When there is a lot of food, adult bears like to play together. They play fight like cubs.

LONE BEARS

A bear claws a tree.
He is marking his land.

Bears have home ranges. They want land that gives them food. They want a safe place to sleep.

Bears mark their land by rubbing on trees. They mark their land by peeing on it.

Sometimes, bears live near other bears. Males and females live close together when they want to make cubs. Bears also share land when there is a lot of food.

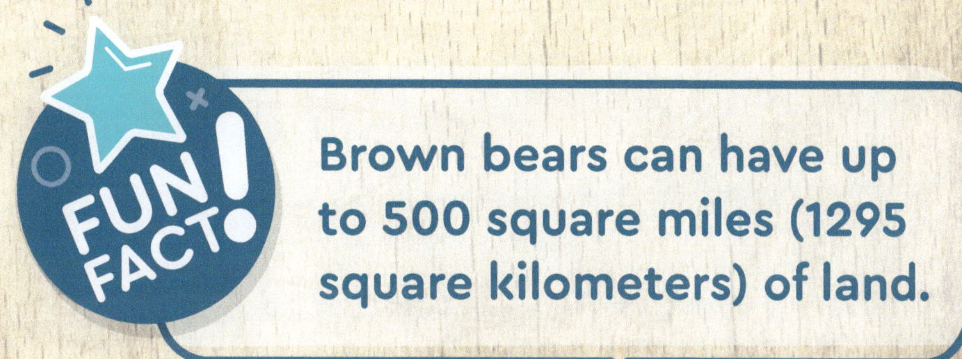

LOSING HOMES

KIDS CAN HELP THE EARTH

A polar bear swims for land, but there is less ice. And the land is far away.

Ice is melting. Forests are getting smaller. People are moving in.

Bears are losing their homes. Polar bears need ice to hunt for seals. Brown and black bears need forests to find food.

But the earth is warming. The ice is melting. And people are cutting down trees. They are building towns. They are building roads.

Bears cannot find as much food. They try to find it in towns. They are hurt by cars. They run into humans.

DO NOT RUN!
DID YOU KNOW?
When bears stand on their back legs, they are just curious.

Hikers freeze. A black bear walks up the path.

If a person sees a bear, they should not run.

When a person sees a brown bear, they should keep an eye on the bear and walk away slowly. If the bear attacks, humans should lie on their stomachs and wait until the bear leaves.

Black bears scare easier. If a black bear attacks, a person should try to look big. They should raise their arms. They should shout. They should use bear spray.

If a human sees a polar bear, they should leave quietly. But if it attacks, they should fight back.

BACK TO
THE WILD

MORE AMAZING ANIMAL BOOKS from Nature Kids Publishing!

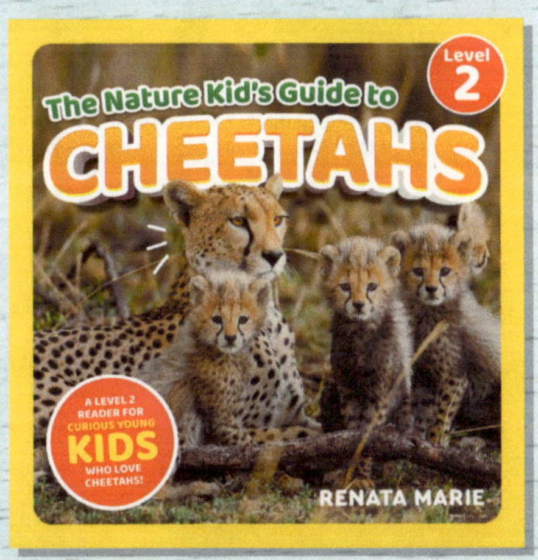

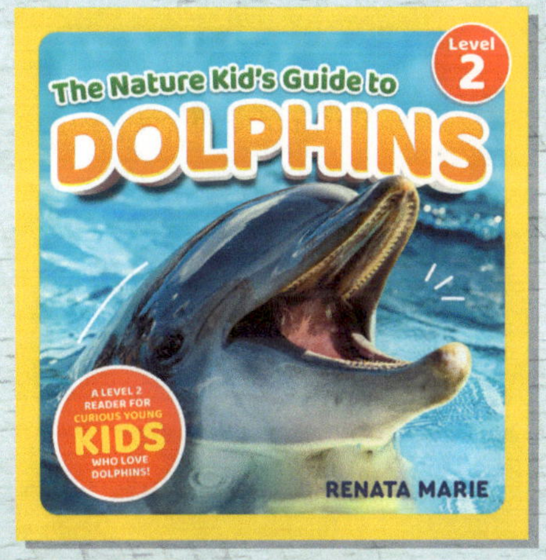

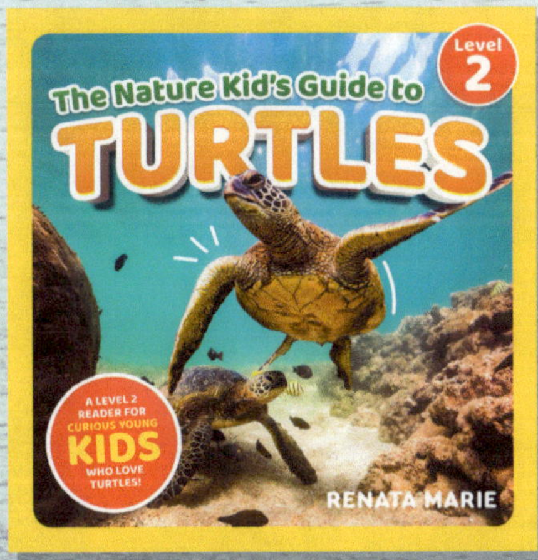

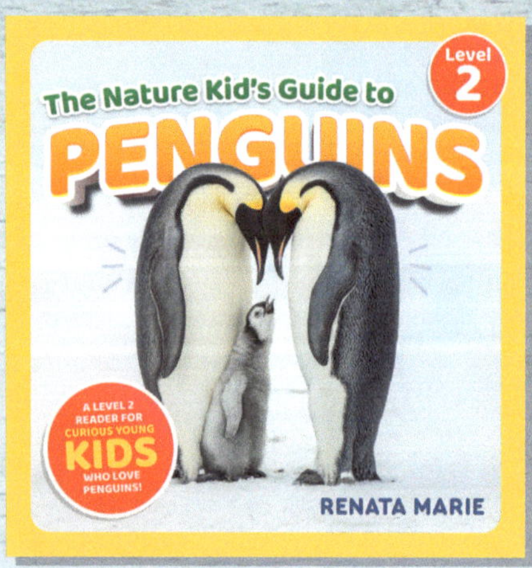

Visit NatureKidsPublishing.com
to Learn More!

www.ingramcontent.com/pod-product-compliance
Lightning Source LLC
Chambersburg PA
CBHW042123030726

47599CB00002B/327

A bear walks away from a town. He is going home to the forest.

People are trying to help the earth. They want the ice and trees to return. They want bears to stay in the wild.

There, they are free to be the big, top predators they were born to be.

People can help keep bears out of towns. They can keep food inside. They can use trash bins that lock to keep bears out.

AROUND THE WORLD
FUN FACT!
Koala bears are not a type of bear, even though they are called bears.
38

A bear digs for bugs.
It is a sloth bear.

Bears live all over the world. Brown bears, black bears, and polar bears live in North America. Brown bears and polar bears also live in Europe and Asia. Giant pandas, moon bears, sun bears, and sloth bears live in Asia too. Spectacled bears live in South America.

No matter where they live, bears are the big hunters of the world.

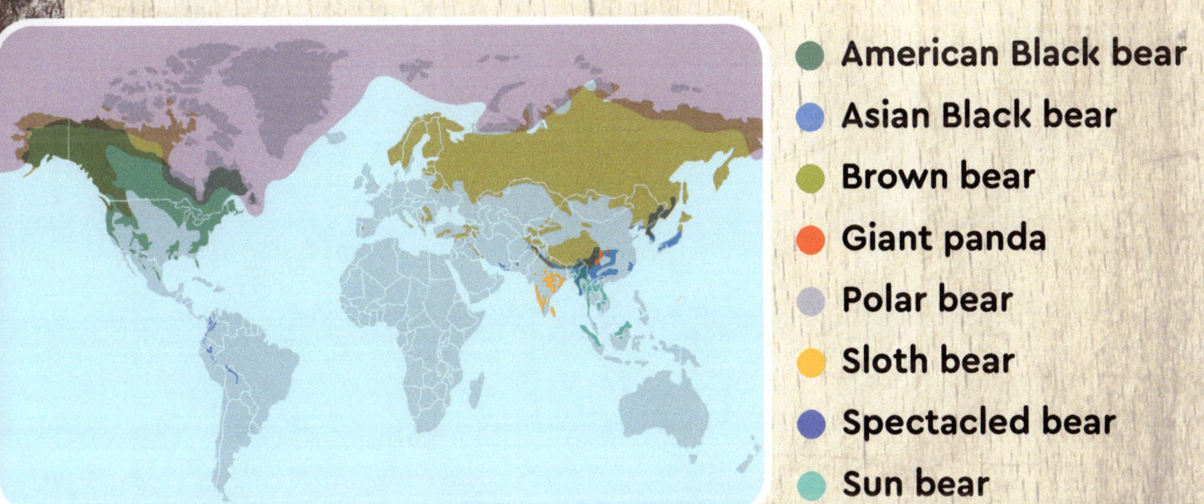

GLOSSARY

growl
to make a low sound
in the throat

page 29

omnivores
animals that eat
plants and meat

page 11

predators
animals that hunt
other animals

page 17

prey
animals that are hunted
by other animals

page 9

wrestle
when animals try to push
each other to the ground

page 27